SPINSTER FOR HIRE

Also by Julia Story:
Post Moxie
The Trapdoor
Julie the Astonishing

Julie + Manuel

spinster for hire

I love you both.

Julia Story

Julie Story

THE WORD WORKS
WASHINGTON, D. C.

THE WORD WORKS
P.O. Box 42164
Washington, D.C. 20015
editor@wordworksbooks.org

Cover art: "Reverie," Gertrude Abercrombie
Used by permission of the Illinois State Museum
Cover design: Susan Pearce Design
Author photograph: Lulu Lovering

ISBN: 978-1-944585-39-6

Acknowledgments

Some of the poems (several in different versions) originally appeared in *Barnstorm*, *Diode*, *Gulf Coast*, *H_NGM_N*, *The New Yorker*, *Mount Island*, *Pangyrus*, *The Pushcart Prize XL: Best of the Small Presses 2016 Edition*, *Rockhurst Review*, *Rove*, *Salamander*, *Sixth Finch*, and *Xavier Review*. They are reprinted here with much gratitude.

Immense thanks to Simeon Berry, Heather Madden, and Sarah Chace who helped with early drafts. Thank you to The Word Works for believing in this book. Thank you to my family for so many things, including nature, dogs, and the absurd. Thank you to Hilfield, Somerville, and Cape Cod: the places where I wrote this. And thank you to Richard for all the lives we've lived.

Contents

For Remedy

The Pain Scale

You ask me every time I come
to give you the definition of this thing

I carry with me, which in so many ways
has gone beyond pain: a burning hand

that takes me to sometimes even a trail
of beauty, to dying trees covered

in scaffolding, a map of crushed stuff
at their feet. The longer I stay and look

the more the distant box opens,
and I can warble or crawl toward it

instead of just trying to sit in this chair.
I don't know how to be here

either, but the longer I make the path,
the more lookouts appear. There is a skull

with light in it, a holy shovel until I'm
nailed again to the sky in my head

and we stand here together like clouds.

Indiana Problem (Alone)

To wake meant
get on the bike,
try every day
to look for a place
to be alone. Some-
times the church,
slowly pedaling up:
on a hill, a smell
of wood smoke,
the sun a stupid
ashtray.

*

On some Sundays
I played clench-
jawed tearful
Bach and outside
the shaky red
of the stained-
glass window I
imagined myself
in one of the new
trees on the hill; or
not in one exactly,
but I imagined
it in its sea of red
air. After church it
was a suburban tree
again with nothing
really to say.

*

Several miles could
take me to the river.
There was often a dead
deer and sometimes
I could see an eagle
in one of the sycamores,
or I would look
and look for an eagle
someone pointed out
to me until finally
I pretended to see it.

Barely There

I had touched the weeping birch in the cemetery so many times that there was a small mark, a grease mark or worn place where my hand had rested, trying to feel the spinning that connected it to some invisible underground pathway. The craniosacral therapist told me it would feel like humming and that the corpses who branched underneath me like a flattened tree would not bother me, would only bring power and courage to the birch and then maybe to me. Across the street from this cemetery is a house I've walked by many times. The family I've asked to populate it, for just a few minutes, is tender, is barely there. A hint of legs on stairs, a see-through coffee cup held by an almost-hand, no coffee going into it. Plants with light shot through them, secret corners with sealike breath. Only the dog is fully there, in the back of the house, sleeping with her head on her white paws. The quiet shuffling of my family waiting for me. I lean away from an invisible hallway, not wanting to touch anything or to destroy what isn't really mine, but how do you move without moving toward things or people. Or why would you move without them.

Three Bodies

A lamb shoulder
cooked in hay.
Other shoulders
cooked or not,
hurting or not,
carrying the head
where it wants.
Toward dead
animals to eat,
dead animals
to inspect for
an answer:
What is inside?
Who hurt you?
Some are all
lungs. Some
have no lungs
and live just
by being here.

*

In the dark
I knock over
the neighbor's
ceramic collie.
The sound is
like a bouquet
hitting dog
fur. But the
nose comes off
and the paw
and I look for
somewhere
to hide them.

*

In one translation
of the Bible, the
word "single"
is used to describe
two eyes that
become one.
When the eye
is single, united
in itself, the body
fills with light. In
another translation,
the eyes must
be good, and then
the body fills
with a different
kind of light.

Indiana Problem (Toad Circus)

The day after my toad circus the toads were all dead, crunchy and silent in their window well. I wanted to draw a doorway to walk through to get to the world of lilacs: purple, contagious green leaves and no movement but the steady invisible breathing of flowers. I knew I had to tell someone what I had done, so I first walked to the park and stayed there until dusk, sitting on the glider or in the middle of the rusty and dangerous merry-go-round; I can't remember which. When it was nearly dark I walked home, certain that they were worried and maybe even out looking for me. When I got there I saw them busy in the kitchen through the window, so I hid in the backyard until it was good and dark, a living thing on a swing set in the gloom, the attic in my head cracking open for the first time and I went in.

Sea Pig

In the distance, what appears to be a black
and white pig is swimming. Sweaty-hearted

and alone, I seep into the underworld
where pigs have taken to water, and I look

down at my hands, two long white things
that live on their own, not to hold or make

but to be found by another startled creature
like me, at dusk or dawn, mistaken at first

for seagulls or trash, but then seen for what
they are: hands. The pig folds itself into

the water and I see only solid gray ocean doing
its impression of the cave-wall sky. Then what I am

emerges grizzled, like a beard grown in captivity.

Monstress

My face: talking signpost
or locked door to a ballroom

in a derelict hotel. I walk
alone through the woods

to the house of another dead
Englishman. There are families

and clots of children exclaiming
over a live cat in a bedroom;

then silent but shoulder-to-shoulder,
they read about 18th century hair.

For all to see I clonk my head
in a tiny doorway, exclaim in

American while everyone looks away.
Before there were humans

there was darkness: dark swaying,
a mist, a lake of blood, but

everything was a lake of blood.
And born of the blood were even

creatures like me, who make mothers
run from every direction, who sleep

as open-hearted as the newly dead.

Indiana Problem (Three Dusks)

Feet sort of
on the ground,
I walked through
the silence of a
clock radio, kid
and dog voices
and some wind
retrieving its
stupidity, flinging
it back into
the dull summer
neighborhood.

*

The trees on
The Hulk
were never
more alive
as they churned
out pure green
bird voices, their
hearts inside-
out ruins, their
eyes connected
to roots that could
speak to both
the living and
the dead.

*

I was scared
that Jesus might
come out of
a cave to make
peace with me,
a gentle stroll
through the sleep-
shaped universe,
the fraction-shaped
universe.

The Well

I couldn't sleep and stayed up most of the night on oxycodone, watching horror movies and placing my body into the weird contortion that turned the pain from a nail gun into a moderately-smoking campfire. Then it was morning and I had to go to the basement but I was too scared. The last time I tried, I fell down the rotting steps and landed with my cheek in a puddle, a displaced bug scurrying by my eyelash. I had stopped going to work and lived in a voice-structure: instead of walls and floors and my third-floor view of roofs, every step seemed to place me on paths of braided invisible limbs as I went from bed to bathroom to hunch over the stove. I heard voices in these creatures, and before long it was easier to stay in bed, folded into my V-shape. For most of my life I couldn't watch horror movies because I believed in real demonic possession, but now I don't mind the stupidity of horror movie people: their underwater movement, their staring and staring into indifferent caverns of nothingness. In one movie the angry dead girl wanted the people to learn a lesson, but what they needed to learn was the worst kind of exhaustion and they wouldn't learn it. They finally found the well under the floor but finding it only made things worse. One ended with no eyes while another was cursed to live this life over and over again.

Spinster for Hire

What's missing is where
our longing is. Standing

under the tree, there isn't
any feeling. Invertebrates

of feeling swim slowly
away from me. I sat all

winter and watched you
from my window. The

procession of cars, feet,
an occasional darting

creature was like a slow-
motion winter-long moth

parade. On my walls
I had nothing but a framed

photograph of a gibbon
and the painting made

for me by the Russian.
You don't need to know

anything else about him
except he was the Russian.

When spring came, I
moved. The rhododendrons

were in bloom in their
dark pathways of half-

medieval air. Deep under-
ground bones turned

to chalk. I packed all
of my things into moldy

boxes and boxes into
the waiting truck. You

all stood there and didn't
help me, but it was all right.

Now I live above the beauty
parlor. The town tries

to sleep again for the winter.
If you look up you can see

me in my window, one spot
of life in our hibernation,

our long orchard of silence.

Today's Alchemy

On a Top of the Pops from 1980,
Phil Collins in his Hawaiian shirt
dances awkwardly, lip synching,
his bald spot flashing pink and blue.
The couch I just bought is already
wearing out and gray dust covers
everything, even the sky and distant
tangle of trees. Out the window I watch
a new lamb unfold onto bent legs.
I feel a pulley in my chest whenever
I look at her movement, crumpled
and blind, automatic. Her pupils
are rectangular like the pupils
of all prey. I could hunt her if
I wanted to. But my natural instinct
is a long Formica counter with a row
of harmless ladies stalking their feelings,
collapsing and stuck in their own black holes.
Phil Collins, my flamingo in flight,
my looped dancer of mediocrity: all I have
is the external. Boys and girls on the greatest day
of their lives dance and push each other
to the stage as the camera swings up to blue
lights before collapsing skin and young joy
into me, their silent mannequin.

Indiana Problem (Three Steaks)

The babysitter
came with a suitcase
full of crap we
liked: old clothes,
naked Barbies with
limbs scratched
by some unknown
girl. We ate TV
dinners: mine rubber
corn, burnt square
of chocolate, spongy
metallic rectangle.

*

At The Camelot
I would eat
the entire prime
rib on its bed
of soggy toast
before taking
my ice cream cone
into the bar
with its full suit
of armor, drunks
I'd recognize
in daylight.

*

I left the charred
fat in a little
wall, left
the camper
and walked into
the firefly-packed
dark green dark and
no one looked
for me.

Picture of a River

They could eat food but it made them decay. I read about it, then put the book down and slept for five hours. I dreamed the river took the dead in a type of passageway, on its way to somewhere else, or toward other people. People were stacked up on the weedy shores, swaying like haphazard piles of books. I saw a picture like this once. In Sunday School Mrs. McIntire passed the postcard around so we could see the rapture: cars crashing on earth, skeletons floating up to heaven, men and women in suits on fire, Jesus' head floating like an egg in the sky. He looked a combination of mean and sorry. Underneath it all in hell the people worked with shovels and picks, hundreds of them on different levels and more descending, their mouths tiny straight lines. The worst thing that could happen was a lifetime of physical labor underground. There were flames but they were small. There was a river full of small boats, and the mouths of the people in the boats were screaming, as if moving through the water instead of shoveling for Satan gave them time to think about eternity. The river here, in the book and in my head, moves part of me to another part of me. There was a river in my town: it did nothing. Time in its own way, awake and asleep, makes something slow I can barely see. It waits like the river of my childhood. It takes the dead away from the dead.

Straw Dogs

To protect nothing with nothing: pretend gunshot
while they film a movie about the real man who
was hunted. The same sofa there, the same TV,

the same sound outside, and a pretend hunted man
in the real streets with our sky, our buildings waiting.
A woman who heard the real gunshot listening

to the pretend gunshot, standing and listening
in a room that is hers, was given to her, is hers.
Then a long psychedelic rape scene. No thanks, but it's

part of the plot. Not the plot of this movie
but a story we believe in which is the story of a
woman who wants to learn to love the pain

she is given. Relaxing into a state of siege,
the sofa gentle at her back, waiting for this to
end and then this and this and this and this.

Heaven and hell take and give, with caring or not
caring. Making people and anything out of trash
and sky, burning it all, making it again, burning it.

Neighborhood

I was tucked away by the laundry machines and the dank room where the landlord kept rusty bikes, fake Christmas trees, abandoned boxes of clothes. I heard the hum and gurgling of the building day and night, mystery clanks, the soft paddings of the tenants with 401ks coming down to wash their clothes. Underneath, the faint and constant sewer. "This is *my* neighborhood," one of the neighbors said after my car window was smashed on the sidewalk. Wordlessly I scooped the blue pieces of glass into my hands while he stood watching with a hose. His son joined him and watched me too. It was getting dark and the yelling and traffic from the street started, and the people without neighborhoods put their harnesses on and tried to walk to corners and back, pacing in the dark because they didn't live anywhere. I tried to unlock the door to the basement with my hands full of glass while they all watched me.

Shades

Once I wrote an essay on the origins of the word "shade," maybe in the context of some Blake poems but I can't remember. In addition to what a tree creates, a shade is an apparition, a ghost, what pheasant hens look like in the grass. When I studied words years ago I saw them as separate from me, nails pounded into an empty house. No one lived there and I walked by it quickly in a new outfit every day, pretending it wasn't there. An old man, a preacher, lived next door. Once he told me he saw someone moving around inside the house. "Maybe it was a bird but it looked like a person. A person running around, jumping off the ceiling, a lady. You should check it out or call the police." I put on my "I am kind but slightly lost" face and walked faster. Now I study nothing. I moved into the house, which I share with pheasants or sheep, fires or rivers of doors. The shades flicker near me still and still I try to reach them. Sometimes my head is in the fire but my eyes are here with me flickering, the same as always, but open.

November Rain

I'm thinking of painting
the bedroom a color called

November Rain, which I
can't discuss without

picturing Slash standing
at the top of a cliff after

the accident, still rocking
even though he's dead

and has no electricity. I
don't want to model

thinking or what memory
does. Mostly I just want

people to listen to me and
then maybe understand me

but I don't even care that
much about being understood.

Underground the trees help
each other: even separate

species send messages to
roots smaller or stranger

than their own and in a way
hold each other before

they plunge from their
underground cliffs, and all

I see are the clacking
branches, leaves trying

again to grow, the music
inside all kinds of things

that I'll get around to
one of these days.

Indiana Bardo

Haunted house, duplex
where the landlord threw out
my bike, limestone box

in the trees, yellow house
with red shutters.
The collie did a fear dance

near the driveway of the 90s
mansion, the electric fence
keeping him from his questions:

Me? You? Help. Food.
I floated in a pool filled
with dead leaves and watched

the green light from the window
on silent afternoons. Even the air
was polite. The opinions of the park

were far away and the dark stairs
to the basement offered themselves
with no strings: come down or don't.

Indiana Problem (Fear, 1983)

In one episode of *Little House*, the brother Albert gets addicted to morphine. Doc Baker tells him to puke and he does and then he's not addicted anymore. Even though after I watched it with Mom I asked her if I could do drugs when I grew up (she said no), I knew I never wanted to go through what Albert did: desperate for his next fix in too-short homemade overalls and feathered hair, barfing all over the bed.

I used to keep myself up at night worrying about drug addiction in general, and also sexual intercourse, ghosts, skeletons, and the devil. I would convince myself that a skeleton was standing next to my bed: sometimes I would see the white of a leg bone through one squinted eye with the thrill of hundreds of sparrows beating my skin and I was the only one in the world who had ever been this afraid. I would get through the day dry-eyed and light with exhaustion before night came with its ghost nurses and dried rubbery corpses from *Ripley's Believe It or Not*. And on another *Little House*, Laura gets lost in the hills and is cared for by some old man. When Pa finally finds her, the desperation to keep her that riots out of him froze me: that you could be that wanted, that someone could want to save you.

Small Wonder

"Alf," I think as I wake
in the dark, feeling
the presence of something
animal and human, familiar
and terrifying, ordinary
and hidden. The dad,
the only human character
I remember, was puny,
fussy: his worry powered
everything, as the antics
of the furry child became
old quickly. On *Small
Wonder*, the robot lived
with the family like a real
girl, not understanding how
to hide her non-humanity.
I don't know if she slept
standing in a closet,
but that's what I
would have wanted.
"Vicky": Victorian, like
the rolling-eyed automata
in pharmacy windows,
peddling kidney elixirs
with their jerking. Sitcom
children: tooth-filled, shrill,
hiding loneliness with lessons
about strangers, not getting
stuck in abandoned
appliances, pot and pills.
And Reagan's huge square
head, a sick ghost but
real, part robot and part
live animal.

Three Summers

At the edge, just
out of the frame,
I see a monkey
tail and part
of a monkey
foot. The rest
of the photo
shows a horse
in a sport coat
being led by
a female hand.

*

The dog called
Plum trots
toward me, alone
on the road
to Manor Farm.
She joins me
for a few yards,
giving sideways
glances, judging.
Then she squeezes
under the fence
and runs through
the field. In the
distance, the other
dog waits for her.

*

My husband fell
in love with his
teacher and married
her instead. I stood
in the empty house
and waited with
the lights off.
Then I went
on the porch
with the cicadas
and dark August
flowers. Bubbles
rose in me over
and over. Grief,
I thought, finally.
But it was joy.
Not marching
or in a parade,
or with lights
or giant eyes.
Like pollen
descending
and darkening,
burying me.

The Romantics

I can't see all of human experience
in a bird's nest and if I were to describe
something as "romantic," most likely
what I mean is "damp." Beauty is less
important to me as the jagged coastline
of my heart stretches out into a long
thin line: more surface area where birds
can rest, where anything can rest. When
I was married I fantasized about calling
the numbers on For Rent signs: "One BR w/
W/D all utilities incl" was a dark, magical wood.
The still and empty windows; the dream
of scratched blank wooden floors and appliances
that were mine, mine, mine; a view through
trees for no face but mine. Now my head
is filled with as many empty houses as I dream
as I creak around their closets, dangerous balconies,
the dark tragic corners of their basements.
There is even one cathedral. I don't worship
there, but sometimes I go inside to listen
to the rain, the grass flattening on the hill,
the bloodthirsty wind.

Doorway

First the terror like a far-off bone, the streets
of veins igniting as I walk to the door,

panic of another face close to mine, a face like
my face: no matter how I try, it won't fall off or be lost.

And the voiceless moment of eyes, a rush of birds,
two things together on the plate: a lonely surf

and turf, two dead things who never meet in real life.
The prairie and the sea, two different butchers, blood

darkening a hidden floor; elsewhere, gasps in a sodden
net. Then time, a door slamming, makes a boat between us.

Indiana Problem (Mousetrap)

Wrapped in an afghan and playing
Mousetrap, I worried that I wasn't
giving enough attention to the stupider
toys: Lite Brite with most of the pieces
missing; life-size Barbie head smeared
with red and blue, forever bruised
and smiling; shoebox of rubber animals.
Boredom was always a dim garden in
the background, a place where twilight
was described by adults, ears stretched
toward the opening notes of sitcoms, eyes
stretched toward the windows and the sketchy
trees, dark Hoosier sadness, the houses
so close we could hear their forks and knives
if we left the door open. I didn't plan this
second kingdom: not exactly in the mind
or the heart but in the dullness between
them, a waiting so long it made another
body in case this one got too lonely.

Fully Human

In the video about melancholy,
sadness is shown as a heart
in a birdcage, a heart in a campfire,
a brain in a frying pan, or a heart
being stabbed with a fork. Then it shows
a sharp-toothed black specter enveloping
a naked man who sits slouched and staring
at his heart, which steams in embers.

I'll be in your field, I'll be your field.
I will swim in your sea of children,
I think as I approach the brown fence.
I love you, I say aloud to no one.
Then I climb over the fence
and walk toward the cows, who
start to move away.

I dreamed about a man made of
preserved skin. He was alive but his
skin was dead, but also somehow
alive. I forgot everything else but how
the skin felt: rubber but with breath
underneath. I knew this even though
I never touched him.

Most lonely one. We can make
a blanket out of the natural world if
we want to. The heart is over, all
over. There is a rule for how to live.

America's Stonehenge

Hungover, we crept around
the stone mazes and huts
while I tried to feel something:
if not the hearts of ancient
European mystics, then that
the past, our past, could be
different through sheer will.
There was a grayness under
the trees though the sun shone
somewhere outside them,
and my mean tall boyfriend
stumbled over the stone path
tiny as a road made for dolls,
then lurched with his to-go
cup and illegally gripped one
of the walls of the caves that
were too small to enter. Even
if we could have stood in them,
there were tall hedgerows in us
with cars scurrying to prevent
that, or dull afternoons in other
cars trying for hours to figure
out where to go before giving
up, or unseen animals underlining
the silence or pacing or just
sitting before wandering into
their pits of sleep. What I see
as the main idea of the real
Stonehenge is that there is no
cleansing or hiding or giving
up; no levels to ascend, no boat
to take us somewhere. A night
with stars waiting is not beyond
our grasp. There are no answers
beyond this stupid wandering.
There are some tall rocks.

Indiana Problem (Time)

The angry pug chased me for
awhile as I rode my bike. Time
turned to a nearly solid light,
a heavy amber. Suspended in it

were late-summer oak and ash trees,
enormous and kindly. I steered the bike
toward the edge of the light, late
and in trouble, dog teeth near my heel.

Instead of fear, time increased its
chambers: in this moment I was also
damply reading in the carpeted living
room with the smells of old candles

and summer street gathering around
me like a body. Held there in the sack
of time I could rest with the road,
the dog, the trees, the dark and feel

the body waving from a distance: me.
The saddest part of leaving was the lack
of other bodies, their sharp flying-off
somewhere into the hive of night.

Boathouse

Maybe twice in my life
I've held an oar.

I went in a kayak
with my sister-in-law

to the small pine-filled
island. The boat

hit the sand and we
stepped out self-

consciously, quietly
scared of the trash

and evidence of sex
and debauchery. We

found a rock to sit
on and ate cherries.

Then we floated back
on waterways made

of reeds and gnats,
trying to speak

or not speaking.

*

The boat of many years
of floating between words

to get to the right word.
The house not a shelter but

floating in your dream
so you can't get in.

*

If Jesus and the devil
exist simultaneously,

does that mean they
are the same? I rehearsed

the question in my
Philosophy of Religion

class the summer I
tried repeatedly to get

Patrick to spend
the night at my

house. The trick
was to ask without

using words. I came
up with this tactic

as I sat on a concrete
bumper block outside

Mighty Mart, my face
numb from drinking

gin out of a to-go
cup. When Patrick

returned with Twizzlers
I tried my plan.

I always planned
questions carefully

before asking them,
or even wrote them

in my notebook
to assess while

other people talked.
Patrick and I were

hungover. He wore
a white tank top

(he would never
beat anyone's wife)

and gently informed
the class of his agnosticism.

Afterwards we went
to the pool and tried

to read Aquinas.
But it was too hot

to think about evil.
If it does exist,

it is so God can
turn it into good.

The light on the water
shimmered like

a Jello cube, the only
clean water in Iowa.

*

Poolhouse: the sad
Midwestern equivalent.

Or the one from *Fast Times
at Ridgemont High*: brown

shag carpet, dim light
from one high-up

window, the removal
of bathing suits,

muffled splashing, shrieks.

*

In the movie of Lawrence's
Maurice, a Merchant Ivory

masterpiece that I watched
no less than 24 times,

the low-class lover of
Maurice sends a telegram:

Meet me at the boathouse
without fail. He fails.

The dusk on the pond,
the English countryside

doing its best to support
all the doomed literary

lovers by providing toolsheds,
dark woods, well-timed

and positioned horses
to pound them over

the soft forest floor,
taking them to places

we never see: the boathouse
door closes, the figures

lower into each other
before the fire. And

the scene changes.

    *

The white house was built
in 1973, same as all

the others on the block.
I never imagined I'd end

up like this: one key
on the ledge above

the door, smelling the ocean
from my desk in a city.

Packed carefully into my
head is childhood: metal

roller skates stolen from
the yard, paper route,

big old men smoking.
Big old cars. Questions

asked and silence
following. Questions

unasked. Screaming "Just
a minute!" the time

the Barbie pool leaked
as I illegally filled it

with water in my room,
one Dixie cup at a time.

The Barbies were enjoying
plastic hot dogs on

a plastic grill. All of those
houses, born the same

year, swelling up with
children, retching them

onto the street where
we fought each other,

chased fireflies, ran
away from home.

*

I rent the sailboat
when it is nearly dark,

when there is little time
left. I don't know how

to do anything, so I sit
and watch the college

student sail us. The water
of the river is dirty, but

it is my water. When
we bring the boat in,

the lights have turned
on, and another college

kid docks it, doesn't
say anything. Then as I

turn to walk away—back to
the car waiting for me,

the dark house—
he says, "Beautiful night."

*

I swam away from
the pontoon, jealous

of my cousin who was
not ugly. I reached the wrong

shore and without glasses
wandered over beaches where

large Iowans blurrily
barbequed and drank.

The sun burned into my
scalp and shoulders—now I

was crying, I thought
I might wander there

for hours—I wandered
for hours. My eyes kept

returning to the lake, where
our boat was swallowed into

the bluish line between
water and sky. Which isn't

really a line at all, just another
blue space where I couldn't be.

Indiana Problem (A Lost Shuttlecock)

When it was dusk
and we played as hard as we
could until we could
no longer see our feet
in the grass.

And the Addams Family
pinball game, when Thing
crept out and the ball
went nowhere.

And the old Ford, the one
longed for and dreaded.
When it appeared, the impatience
at its ordinariness, how it
arrived out of the recesses
of all the lost things
and then just sat there.

Indiana Problem (Mini Gym)

Whitesnake blasting, the three
girls high on eight cans of Jolt

each fell into the mini gym,
shrieking in voices that said

*I am shrieking. Please. I am
shrieking.* Aquanet, the lights

off, me heading for the small
yellow girls' room to feel

bad in a stall. I didn't shriek
but I imagined myself as

someone who would, some-
one who could make people

stop and look with my voice
alone. When it was time

for the fireworks no one came
to look for me, so with heart

pounding I stood by the glass
door under the fluorescent

lights, frozen in the fear that
someone would turn and see

me and in my box watched
the silent wild explosions

that were like thousands of fists.

Sublime

Yes, that example of death and destruction
is exactly what I'm talking about. That sounds
truly sublime. There must be a hint of death
in it, but over and over no one wants to talk
about death, and what do I know about it
anyway.

I pace the room with a biscotti, remembering
this. My own pain and suffering: too scared
to go to the beach alone. The pain like everything
I love thrown into the trees. *Misunderstood*.

I've changed my stance: you should probably
keep your children away from me. Lying on
the deck for a quick nap, I come to in a restaurant,
seated at a reasonable distance from those
who have not forgotten to not be alone.

I am about to hit all of the hard parts of my body
on some unforgiving street, but instead I land
on another body, and another. All of the bodies
surrounding me: not piled up, but stacked neatly,
facing me, waiting for me.

Domincula

Badger holes
are everywhere,
dark sarcophagi
in reverse,
filled with
violent sleeping
mammals.

In a field
there's a bell;
not for church
because there is
no church.
You can ring it
if you choose,
and if you are
alone, you can
listen to it alone.

Indiana Problem (Dollhouse)

The dollhouse people had wire
inside their arms and legs. I wanted
to live in there. A scrap of our olive
green rug could be their rug,
a toothpaste cap could be something,
or a dandelion.

I squatted on the driveway, singing
and showing off to someone. I lost my
balance and pitched forward onto
my chin. The blood was like a dog
finally ripping his chain loose. There
was no one home so I went in to stretch
out on the couch alone in the late summer
darkness, a wad of Kleenex glued
to my chin, and imagined a white coffin,
a room of people crying for a child.
No one I knew.

Indiana Problem (Covenant)

Every Maundy Thursday they turned off all the lights at church while a deacon yelled "Crucify him!" from the balcony. Once it scared me so much I cried, guilty over my role in the demise of the kind dead person who wanted to be my friend. Everyone in my town hated me for reasons I never understood, and once when I was twelve and was taking organ lessons from the music director who was mean to me but nice to everyone else, I waited under the yield sign by the sanctuary to get picked up and a little boy rode up on his bike. He circled the parking lot, crunching through the early fall leaves, the sky blue with the hope available to all sinners, and stared at me while I tried to arrange myself in an inoffensive way. Then he rode off easily, laughing, as if I were a joke too stupid to respond to or try to understand.

Husbandry

The working cocker mounts my 10-pound dachshund; earlier he humped his great-grandmother. It's for once not raining, and the two dogs are lit up from behind by the setting sun, the dying-Muppet sheep sounds so loud that we have to keep saying What? The ram is soon to be outfitted with a crayon that will mark the ewes he mates with because most of the lambs in the field were surprises. Though the ghosts of many farmers stand within me, I'm more Monsanto and McMansion-spotted bean fields than what is bred here. When I was a tired divorcee in Indiana, women young and old stood mightily between me and their husbands, afraid that when I stopped being sad I would be ready to mate. Now breeding permeates the air like an ocean of ground squirrels I saw once: writhing and undulating, each separate, but swarmed together into a sheet of tribal, comforted fur.

Of Use

It was dark and I tripped on the dog stairs
on the way to the bathroom. The dog
needs stairs to get on the bed because
her legs are so short. I was in the basement
and saw the rain hit the grass in the dark
through the window, lit up by headlights.
I was at worm level. As a woman, I am
closer to being an animal than a man is.
The dog moved over in the bed so I could
get back in. Closer to animals, I am more
prone to Satan. I am more easily seduced
by the things that cast shadows. It's how
you know I'm not dead. A long time ago,
and maybe even now, the gods did horrible
things because they could. But even in the
journey through purgatory there is day
and night, friendly dead orators, mountain-
side rest, brooks, insane skies, green angels,
fields of gentle monsters and their stories. And
within the owl is the process to make its
pellet, the capsule of the stuff it doesn't need:
a little package of bones and fur that must be
of some use to something. In the morning
I was still underground but could leave if I
wanted, could walk the sidewalks where most
people seemed to be pregnant. The guy still
had my coffee. I could stand for a long time
and watch a horse in a field above ground.
There was ground in the place I asked for,
and in its way, it needed me.

Indiana Problem (After John Yau)

In the photo of me outside the airport I am wearing pink: glasses, skirt, woven belt, shoes. The tree I touch is not wearing leaves, only the pale green light of future leaves. Together we are a statue that represents the end of "childhood" as we know it. See how the braces glint in the sun, the eyes move cementward. Behind the camera there is no love, only a desire to end each moment before it arrives. All of us together—me, tree, camera, moment—are in this box. Even you, the hands that put it away and forgot it, are inside these bodies we make: the one that remembers while the other moves toward the disappearing planes.

New England Bardo

Fragile spring light is a tangled branch song.

A loud college student in pink shorts. Remember
how I went out to save that baby rabbit? he asks
the barista. Well, guess what Megan just told me.
That baby bunny was eaten by a cat.

The smell of paint and dust-spiders.

Close your eyes: the white outline of a choir
boy in robes, pointing toward the window.

Moth

I took a long walk
to the end of the arm,
to the lighthouse.

People don't live in them
anymore but a man
did live in this one.

I say man but he
was half-man, half-rabbit—
a satyr but shorter

and he couldn't jump.
He just reminded me
of a rabbit. All night

the light swept
over the black water
like God saying Here, here

is what I have for you.
And I didn't like it
so I looked at the gray

wood floors, specked
with salt and dirt.
The man didn't have

anything to look at
but the windows,
so he looked out.

I took a hidden staircase
back to the earth
and I swam a few feet

in the dark until I was tired.
When I made my way
back down the arm

it was many months later
and no one could see me
because I had turned

part moth. I went back
to my house and lived
the rest of my days

near the spines of the people
who came looking for me,
or I hid in the walls,

white and dusty. There is
no one to hear me say it
and there is no voice

to say it with: I was loved.

The New Trinity

The computer asks if I'm sure I want to open a demon. Maybe?
Cancel. It is still quiet; I am still alone, with enough time each
day to wonder what my function is. To dig bodies out of the
ashes to write down. To keep a small dog body alive. To keep
this larger human body here and talking. How much of a liver
do I need? And what about the soul? It would be easier if I still
saw soul and spirit connected: a double cartoon ghost which
could enter and exit easily, the body a shaggy disc drive. What
is spirit? Drinks that give life? Or a light shining above the
weary eyes of the Lord. Soul is further down: the voice getting
deeper, the body moving further away, turning more red and
like blood, solid blood that moves quietly, like a kite in a bed of
wind. And where do demons fit in, should they find their way?
A new trinity of friends, because why shouldn't I befriend the
demon? Holding hands around the campfire that was once my
heart and is now a home for wayward others.

The Illuminated World

Thanks to Edison, Victorian times were half dark
and half light: a wall knocked down, and people

shrank from the brightness which turned adults
to haggard specters, babies to preternatural

homunculi, and the previously shadowed streets
to fields of terror, every roach and criminal

scurrying. Before the dark was knocked away,
light was a river, brown and soundless, moving

into space like an unwound spiral. And citizens
crept in their dark spaces like hermits in their

anchor-holds: a candle or gaslight to show them
their world one object at a time. Too much light

too quickly makes me run also: in the field of myself
there are no night games, just a quick run around

the dark bases at dusk, carnivores lurking. And when
I'm a room, I walk around it with my own flashlight;

my hands are flashlights. There isn't much to read.
The door is closed. I wave my hands.

And the Waters Prevailed

The golf course is flooded again;
a dead deer floats in the Wabash.
The smell of the corn syrup plant
is pretty much what you'd expect:
burnt corn with a hint of cotton candy,
but also something underneath that.
A death, but not human or animal.
A general death. Indiana: death in general.

The repetitions that occur in nature
are boring today. One spiral on top of
another, the rain adding nothing but more
rain to its monologue about rain.
Underneath its constant muttering
is the anthem of the ground: Until further
notice, I'm alive.

About the Author

Julia Story is the author of *Post Moxie* (Sarabande Books) and the chapbooks *The Trapdoor* (dancing girl press) and *Julie the Astonishing* (Sixth Finch Books). Her work has been awarded a Pushcart Prize and has appeared in many publications including *Gulf Coast*, *Ploughshares*, *The Paris Review*, *Diode*, and *The New Yorker*. She is from Indiana and now lives in Massachusetts.

About the Artist

Gertrude Abercrombie (1909-1977) was an American painter known for her Surrealist work. Born in Austin, TX, she traveled with her parents around America and Europe as they worked for an opera company. She studied at the University of Illinois and the School of the Art Institute Chicago. Abercrombie's works are held in the collections of the Smithsonian American Art Museum, the Milwaukee Art Museum, and the Museum of Contemporary Art in Chicago, among others.

ABOUT THE WORD WORKS

Since its founding in 1974, The Word Works has steadily published volumes of contemporary poetry and presented public programs. Its imprints include The Washington Prize, The Tenth Gate Prize, The Hilary Tham Capital Collection, and International Editions.

Monthly, The Word Works offers free literary programs in the Café Muse series at the Writers Center in Bethesda, MD, and each summer it holds free poetry programs in Washington, D.C.'s Rock Creek Park. Word Works programs have included "In the Shadow of the Capitol," a symposium and archival project on the African American intellectual community in segregated Washington, D.C.; the Gunston Arts Center Poetry Series; the Poet Editor panel discussions at The Writer's Center; Master Class workshops; and a writing retreat in Tuscany, Italy.

As a 501(c)3 organization, The Word Works has received awards from the National Endowment for the Arts, the National Endowment for the Humanities, the D.C. Commission on the Arts & Humanities, the Witter Bynner Foundation, Poets & Writers, The Writer's Center, Bell Atlantic, the David G. Taft Foundation, and others, including many generous private patrons.

The Word Works is a member of the Community of Literary Magazines and Presses and its books are distributed by Small Press Distribution.

wordworksbooks.org

OTHER WORD WORKS BOOKS

Annik Adey-Babinski, *Okay Cool No Smoking Love Pony*
Karren L. Alenier, *Wandering on the Outside*
Karren L. Alenier, ed., *Whose Woods These Are*
Karren L. Alenier & Miles David Moore, eds.,
     Winners: A Retrospective of the Washington Prize
Christopher Bursk, ed., *Cool Fire*
Willa Carroll, *Nerve Chorus*
Grace Cavalieri, *Creature Comforts*
Abby Chew, *A Bear Approaches from the Sky*
Nadia Colburn, *The High Shelf*
Henry Crawford, *The Binary Planet*
Barbara Goldberg, *Berta Broadfoot and Pepin the Short*
Akua Lezli Hope, *Them Gone*
Frannie Lindsay, *If Mercy*
Elaine Maggarrell, *The Madness of Chefs*
Marilyn McCabe, *Glass Factory*
Kevin McLellan, *Ornitheology*
JoAnne McFarland, *Identifying the Body*
Leslie McGrath, *Feminists Are Passing from Our Lives*
Ann Pelletier, *Letter That Never*
Ayaz Pirani, *Happy You Are Here*
W.T. Pfefferle, *My Coolest Shirt*
Jacklyn Potter, Dwaine Rieves, Gary Stein, eds.,
     Cabin Fever: Poets at Joaquin Miller's Cabin
Robert Sargent, *Aspects of a Southern Story*
     & *A Woman from Memphis*
Julia Story, *Spinster for Hire*
Miles Waggener, *Superstition Freeway*
Fritz Ward, *Tsunami Diorama*
Camille-Yvette Welsh, *The Four Ugliest Children in Christendom*
Amber West, *Hen & God*
Maceo Whitaker, *Narco Farm*
Nancy White, ed., *Word for Word*

THE WASHINGTON PRIZE

Nathalie Anderson, *Following Fred Astaire*, 1998

Michael Atkinson, *One Hundred Children Waiting for a Train*, 2001

Molly Bashaw, *The Whole Field Still Moving Inside It*, 2013

Carrie Bennett, *biography of water*, 2004

Peter Blair, *Last Heat*, 1999

John Bradley, *Love-in-Idleness: The Poetry of Roberto Zingarello*, 1995,
      2ND edition 2014

Christopher Bursk, *The Way Water Rubs Stone*, 1988

Richard Carr, *Ace*, 2008

Jamison Crabtree, *Rel[AM]ent*, 2014

Jessica Cuello, *Hunt*, 2016

Barbara Duffey, *Simple Machines*, 2015

B. K. Fischer, *St. Rage's Vault*, 2012

Linda Lee Harper, *Toward Desire*, 1995

Ann Rae Jonas, *A Diamond Is Hard But Not Tough*, 1997

Annie Kim, *Eros, Unbroken*, 2019

Susan Lewis, *Zoom*, 2017

Frannie Lindsay, *Mayweed*, 2009

Richard Lyons, *Fleur Carnivore*, 2005

Elaine Magarrell, *Blameless Lives*, 1991

Fred Marchant, *Tipping Point*, 1993, 2ND edition 2013

Nils Michals, *Gembox*, 2018

Ron Mohring, *Survivable World*, 2003

Barbara Moore, *Farewell to the Body*, 1990

Brad Richard, *Motion Studies*, 2010

Jay Rogoff, *The Cutoff*, 1994

Prartho Sereno, *Call from Paris*, 2007, 2ND edition 2013

Enid Shomer, *Stalking the Florida Panther*, 1987

John Surowiecki, *The Hat City After Men Stopped Wearing Hats*, 2006

Miles Waggener, *Phoenix Suites*, 2002

Charlotte Warren, *Gandhi's Lap*, 2000

Mike White, *How to Make a Bird with Two Hands*, 2011

Nancy White, *Sun, Moon, Salt*, 1992, 2ND edition 2010

George Young, *Spinoza's Mouse*, 1996

THE HILARY THAM CAPITAL COLLECTION

Nathalie Anderson, *Stain*
Mel Belin, *Flesh That Was Chrysalis*
Carrie Bennett, *The Land Is a Painted Thing*
Doris Brody, *Judging the Distance*
Sarah Browning, *Whiskey in the Garden of Eden*
Grace Cavalieri, *Pinecrest Rest Haven*
Cheryl Clarke, *By My Precise Haircut*
Christopher Conlon, *Gilbert and Garbo in Love*
        & *Mary Falls: Requiem for Mrs. Surratt*
Donna Denizé, *Broken Like Job*
W. Perry Epes, *Nothing Happened*
David Eye, *Seed*
Bernadette Geyer, *The Scabbard of Her Throat*
Elizabeth Gross, *this body / that lightning show*
Barbara G. S. Hagerty, *Twinzilla*
Lisa Hase-Jackson, *Flint & Fire*
James Hopkins, *Eight Pale Women*
Donald Illich, *Chance Bodies*
Brandon Johnson, *Love's Skin*
Thomas March, *Aftermath*
Marilyn McCabe, *Perpetual Motion*
Judith McCombs, *The Habit of Fire*
James McEwen, *Snake Country*
Miles David Moore, *The Bears of Paris* & *Rollercoaster*
Kathi Morrison-Taylor, *By the Nest*
Tera Vale Ragan, *Reading the Ground*
Michael Shaffner, *The Good Opinion of Squirrels*
Maria Terrone, *The Bodies We Were Loaned*
Hilary Tham, *Bad Names for Women* & *Counting*
Barbara Ungar, *Charlotte Brontë, You Ruined My Life*
        & *Immortal Medusa*
Jonathan Vaile, *Blue Cowboy*
Rosemary Winslow, *Green Bodies*
Kathleen Winter, *Transformer*
Michele Wolf, *Immersion*
Joe Zealberg, *Covalence*

INTERNATIONAL EDITIONS

Kajal Ahmad (Alana Marie Levinson-LaBrosse, Mewan Nahro
      Said Sofi, and Darya Abdul-Karim Ali Najin, trans., with
      Barbara Goldberg), *Handful of Salt*
Liliana Ancalao (Seth Michelson, trans.), *Women of the Big Sky*
Keyne Cheshire (trans.), *Murder at Jagged Rock: A Tragedy*
      by Sophocles
Jeannette L. Clariond (Curtis Bauer, trans.), *Image of Absence*
Jean Cocteau (Mary-Sherman Willis, trans.), *Grace Notes*
Yoko Danno & James C. Hopkins, *The Blue Door*
Moshe Dor, Barbara Goldberg, Giora Leshem, eds., *The Stones*
      Remember: Native Israeli Poets
Moshe Dor (Barbara Goldberg, trans.), *Scorched by the Sun*
Laura Cesarco Eglin (Jesse Lee Kercheval and Catherine Jagoe,
      trans.), *Reborn in Ink*
Vladimir Levchev (Henry Taylor, trans.), *Black Book of the*
      Endangered Species
Marko Pogačar (Andrea Jurjević, trans.), *Dead Letter Office*
Lee Sang (Myong-Hee Kim, trans.) *Crow's Eye View: The Infamy*
      of Lee Sang, Korean Poet

THE TENTH GATE PRIZE

Jennifer Barber, *Works on Paper*, 2015
Lisa Lewis, *Taxonomy of the Missing*, 2017
Brad Richard, *Parasite Kingdom*, 2018
Roger Sedarat, *Haji As Puppet*, 2016
Lisa Sewell, *Impossible Object*, 2014